Tying a Poem

Lawrence Desautels

PublishAmerica
Baltimore

First printing

ISBN: 1-4137-5572-0
PUBLISHED BY PUBLISHAMERICA, LLLP
www.publishamerica.com
Baltimore

Printed in the United States of America

To Lucie . . . who taught me poetry works.
And to Greg and Caralyn, stars I can hold.

Table of Contents

Beara Poems/County Cork '04

Buffalo Poems/New York '03

Beara Poems
County Cork '04

Morning Fire

With a new fire,
strong with peat and coal,
banked to chase the
wet wind
beyond the mountain,
I move my table
from its place
where it faced the sea
to near the hearth,
to rest now,
to stare into the
yellow-orange dancers
as they leap
to follow the smoke
into the morning sky.

The smell of earth,
of grasses and flowers
long dead,
but now free
in the smoke
of the peat,
mixes strong
with the words
as they leave my pen
and trail on the
white page
close now to the heat
of the flames
breathing heavily,

taking life from
the Irish earth
cut and dried
from the same
mountain side
that now gathers the rain
as it moves to the west.

Years from now,
when I dig these words
from mountains
left by my hand,
will they fuel a fire
and bring back to me
the smell of peat smoke,
the sound of the wind,
the feel of the cold rain
as it moves beyond
the mountain to the sea?
Will they bring back
the reels and the jigs,
the tastes and smells
of the pubs,
the farms,
the damp famine cottages
that sink into the earth
to become the mountain
once again?
Will these words
bring back
Ireland?

After the Rain at Anam Cara

Some see storms as metaphors,
raging on the fen, commanded tears
from a disappointed heaven
who speaks in wild tongues
from hillsides to those
who trace the dismal rain
with slanted lines on a dry page.

Such as I, though, will follow the front,
reluctant feet stepping and sliding
to where the hill-spill joins the swift brook.
Sunshine and rain make glittering spears
as one pours down and the other clears,
a struggle in the tail of the storm
that moves in thundering gray to the sea.

Swollen below the cascade now drowns
the gurgles and plashes and trickles,
the whispers of but an hour before.
Soon torrent will return to soft springs,
and I, too refreshed, will take
the useful trouble of the rain
as something less than, but quite like renewal.

The Swimmer

I followed a trout
Up
A
Stream
To-
Day.
I stayed back a bit
Low along the bank,
Stepping over and through
Stone and bush
As it fought
From pool to pool,
Desperate
To reach the lake above.
My destination, too,
I thought,
So why not?
He will lead the way.
(For surely it must be
A he, for only a he
Would risk
This track to chase
Some fin and tail!)

With just smooth water
Before the stony deep
He stopped to rest
Under
A stone bridge,
Shadowed now
From the high sun.

I rested, too,
The climb
Taking from me
As it had
From him,
But my goal less
By nature
Than by sport.

I stood above,
Trying to hide
My curiosity.
But being what it is,
My curiosity
Struck out
On its own
Casting its shadow
On the clear shallows
And gravel bottom
Chasing the trout
To
Deep
W
A
T
E
R.

How a fish so brave
Could find fear
In a shadow,
My most harmless
Appendage,
I can not know.

But he was gone
And I
A
Lone.

I sat,
I reflected.
I reflected
On the water and on you.

And this I do know:

If you were to climb
To the rooftop
And wait for me,
Blue eyes against
Blue sky,
They might tie my feet,
Tie my hands behind
Like a TV criminal,
And still I could
Hop and flop
Up the stairs,
Up the stone,
Up the shakes,
Somehow up
Over
The hang,
To lie with you
On the hot roof.

I hope the trout
Found its mate.

The "Out-my-window" Trilogy

Morning

In midnight's rest
I see Eyeries beyond
The fields and walls—
An angel's canvas.
I wake, to find it there
Once more,
Proof that dreams listen,
Then paint the coming dawn.

Noon

On hillside you're chewing with ease,
You moo and you crap as you please.
    Little did I know,
    What you're doing below
Was starting to make Milleens Cheese.

Seamus O'Seamus (the Kerry poet known as 'The Redundant Pundant'): "If i' taint worthy of a limerick, i' taint worthy."

Night

This penned kiss
will last the
night
to draw us
together
'til

graceful waves
carry you
here.

Now
draw a circle
with your arms
'round
your waist;
close your eyes;
put your ear
to the wind.
In this way
each night
I sneak back
to rest, beside you.

Refuge

I stared beyond the window,
to the great black cliffs
and the settling mist.
"It looks lonely out there."

The man named Finbar
turned to me first:
"The wailing winter winds
put roaring on the sea,
but that is just a kiss
you hear now, lad."

"So it is, to be sure,"
and the door closed
behind the voice
of a newcomer
who stepped
into the pub
taking a seat
facing the fire,
knee-high Wellies
stretched
to the orange heat
of peat and coal
and wood flames.

"Ye'll be late for the cable car
Danny Duff, if you sit
with this rabble."
The bartender spoke
without rising.

"I'll be stayin' for the storm.
and a Paddy will protect me
from hearing about the sea
from a man who sails it from
a mountain farm."

I waited for the others,
for their response
to the stranger,
then joined in their laughter.
For an outsider
must not choose a side
if it can be avoided.

Out there,
beyond the cliff-fall
to the sea,
the rugged, weeping,
bold, purple hillsides
of Dursey Island
have been curtained
by a gray gale that drove
the withered and even
the weathered
to the hearth.

And I nodded
that I would stand
another round.

And Danny Duff
faced us now,
from his chair across the room,
wet back to the fire's heat,

and tipped to me his hat—
"It's a rare thing
to find a good man
on a tall stool—
a welcomed rare thing it is."

And as night edged the day,
adding darkness to the gray,
we shared Guinness and whiskey
in quiet communion
until even the storm had enough
and we went our ways
beneath a starred sky.

Dance Night at Causkey's

The spinning and twirling,
the quick stepping
of the evening
carry us toward midnight.
Soon we will
stand in reverence
as the first notes
of Amhran na bhFiann
replace the waltzes
and the fox trots.

But for now the room
smokes, drinks, dances.

My courage comes
from the nest of pints
that grows with the hours.
And I dance,
my partner patient.
"Good man," she says
and leads me
blind, bat-like,
missing walls
and feet and tables
round the small
dance
floor.
"Good man," she repeats
and we laugh.

I confess:
I practiced the two-step,
alone,
in the kitchen,
on the mountain.

But now I retreat
from a slipjig,
its complex time
too much
for my rock and roll rhythms.

And it would be the last dance
before the Soldier's Song.
And we stand, and sing,
or just move our lips
in Irish, or in imagined Irish.
And there are tears,
always there are tears.
And I carry them
away with me
into the night,
and leave my footprints,
stepped and shuffled,
in Causkey's floor.

Separation Poem

Because I can close my eyes
and smile, and you'll be there
sitting in place, yesterday,
I won't agonize farewell.

And though it's a long, long way
to the bogs, hills, and mountains,
it won't take but a short skip
(or maybe a kick 'n' jig)
of imagination
to bring us together again.

Mona Lisa's Confession

There's a small speck
in the corner of the Mona Lisa,
up high, near the top left.
A flawed stroke,
it's been called,
a dab of dark
hardened
before the Master
stroked it smooth.
I've been up close,
before the guard
could take me roughly
to the side,
to explain
why I could not stand
so near the Dame.

But before he could
she whispered to me
il segreto della macchia—
the secret of the stain.
(I was shocked then
as you are now!)
"Leo," she had said
for that is what she called him.
"I must take a break
and have a pee."
(It would have taken
far too long to say
"Leonardo DaVinci

I must take a break
and have a pee,"
for she had been
sitting for long hours
of strong Italian coffee.)
"I was strung out
on Caffeine
and had to take a pee."
She told me this in Italian,
which is a beautiful language
but rhymes too much
for my pen.

"Much of that morning
a fly buzzed
about the room."
(We like to think
he painted in a studio,
but it was just a room,
with no screens
to the street below.
Once a bird flew in,
she whispered,
and landed on her head.
They both laughed
and quit for the day.)

"But today it was just a fly."
(For those frozen in paint,
every day is 'today.')

"Mo" (for that was
his pet name for her)
"while you are about
your piss, I will

assassinate
(for he liked big words)
that fly."
He had invented a fly swatter
earlier that week
and went to his notes.
But he had misplaced them,
lost now among the plans
for helicopters and tanks—
his 'big kahunas,' he called them.

So he took his brush
and took a swat
just as the fly passed
the canvas
and pinned it there.
Now
stuck,
helpless,
it died.

"Una morte piccola!"
he proclaimed,
and left it there.

Mo returned to
her chair,
replacing the mantle
over her
bare breasts
and shoulders.

He liked to watch
her naked,
crossing the room,

large dark nipples
moving
with the rhythms
of her gait.
Today they bounced
more than usual.

"There must be a way . . ."
he mused.

But Mo's smile
brought him back,
that knowing,
patient smile.

"Leo, the light's
getting bad,
my back's killing me,
and it's sweltering in here."

Leonardo's mind
raced with possibilities.
'Behind every problem
is a possibility' he would say
to anyone who would listen.

But the brush and pallet
in his hand
brought him back
to the canvas.

"Now sit
my pretty.
You have been
distracted —

I can see it
in your eyes—
they've been everywhere
but here.
I don't think
I'll ever get them right."

Of course she told me this all very fast;
she knew they would take me away.
And my Italian is very bad,
and while she was whispering
two French navy officers
spoke very loudly
up near the restraining rope.
I heard the one say
"It appears as if
someone is doing her
a favor from behind."

Is that any way
to talk about a lady?

To a Daffodil, Still and Alone

I can't be sure
but I think it likes me.
This morning
I woke to find
it staring
from its place
on my desk.

Two days ago
it barely
acknowledged
my presence,
while I hung my clothes,
bounced lightly on the bed,
placed my computer
near its cup.

Yesterday I thought
I saw it peeking
round, stretching
its stem to
see what I had to say
as I did my
two-fingered
step-dance—
Lord of the Keyboard
I am, I am!

Today I remain coy,
pretending not to notice

its—no, HER interest.
I look from screen
to hillside beyond
the window,
to the houses and hills,
to the bay beyond;

I check my nails,
count the knots
on one board above
my head—
twenty-six—
all the time
stealing secret
glances,
flirting openly
with her openness.

Yesterday I walked
to Eyeries,
right arm brushing
against raucous
gorse that tried to
get my attention
by scratching messages on
my sleeve.
Scattered in the rock walls
Daffodils cluster.
I wonder where
she lived
before being placed
on my desk
to live lonely
between the freedom

of the fields
and the freedom
of my tap, tap, tapping,
Lordlike on my keyboard.

I stretch,
and like a teenage boy
pull her close,
to let her see
that I have noticed,
to let her see
that I too
can turn from
the freedom
of the hillside
to adapt,
rootless,
to explore
possibility.

Making the Bed

Each morning we rise
Together,
Facing the other,
Bed, acres of bed,
Between.
We sweep our Dreams aside
And fold and tuck
In manners
Practiced and profound:
Your sheets tight and smooth,
And mine, arumple—
An easy slide at night
To be with you again,
No form to disrupt but yours.

This, our
Morning ritual,
A dance
Practiced and profound.

Yet here I rise alone.

If loneliness has no words
Then it speaks through
Actions, singular and silent.
I stand and face the bed,
Without you,
Without your sweeps and folds,
So I leave the bed unmade,
For loneliness has no order.

And on the floor
My shirt and pants remind me
Of those mornings when
We woke to see
Our clothes together
Where they crept
To mingle
While we had love above
On our two-made bed.

Roadsong

(Composed on the road to Castletownbere from Eyeries)

Was something 'bout the day
That made me wander,
That made meander
Ing the thing
To do when duty called.

Was something in the way
The falls was churlin',
That made me grab my
Pack and walk
The road below.

It's always in the air,
This tuggin' whisper,
That calls my spirit
Forth to roam;
It's always in the air,
This singin' siren,
That pulls me forth
Then leads me home
Again.

(like life, a song in progress)

Cutting Poetry

I wash the coal dust
from my hands,
having been to the bin
to fill the bucket,
the black iron bucket
as black as the coal
I would carry to
make the fire
hot beneath the blocks
of brown peat,
and would cook,
as it were,
not one nation,
but two.

Fine Polish Coal
it says on the bag.
And who am I
to doubt,
who washes once,
then twice
to take the fine dust
left by the Fine Coal
from my hands
I was so careful
to keep clean
as I turned
and twisted
the white sack
against the

hard wall of the
blackened box
that held Poland
dug from beneath
the ground by men
blackened on the skin
and within
by that which now
sucks the damp
from the stone
of the hearth
and the rain-wet air.

The peat leaves
nothing on my hands
as I place
another block
upon the flame.
But deep in my lungs
the smoke and the smell
burns what will be
the fields and the walls,
when I dig down
through the bogs
of yesterday
placing each block
to dry, to season,
line after line
on the hillside
of memory.

To Pat Ingoldsby, Dublin Street Poet Esq.

You weren't hard to find, Pat,
sharing space as you were
with Trinity and the Bank of Ireland.

I passed twice,
unsure how to approach
though vowing not to be
one of those promising to
"Catch you on the way back, Pat."

I stopped, turned, stopped, stepped.

Just then a suit
stopped-stepped
between us.

"Mr. Ingoldsby,
could you please move
your place of business
for the Bank feels
you a distraction for what we do."

Street drama I thought:
Would it be
"We don't give a Bollix"
or
"I couldn't give a flying fuck"?

Instead, with a tip of your hat,
"Sir, could you please move
your bank for we—my muse and me—
feel it a distraction for what we do."

I returned the next day.
The bank was gone.
I bought one of everything
you were selling…
including a plastic leprechaun
that danced to "The Eavesdropper"
and "Katie Come Down from Limerick."

You earned it.

Poet's Notebook: Hiking the Eyeries Strand

"Seaweed, shells, and sheepshit!
How a lamb becomes a sheep
I'll never know,
considering most of what they eat,
they leave below."

"Lamb Futures:
Rack of Sweaters
Or Rack of Lamb—
Shorn or Savory,
Naked or Dead."

Me—"Are you Michael James?"
Farmer—"Near enough."

Language as plumage:
Me—"If I dressed better, or had feathers,
    I wouldn't be
    effin' and blindin' and whinjin
    this fucking rain."
Farmer—"So why don't you lie down
    and die dacent!"

Me—"I hear you pour the slowest pint in Cork."
Publican—"You in a hurry, 'ave an 'alf."
Patron—"And if you want to be keepin' it cold, put it near
    my ex-wife's heart."

Me—" I'm freezing. That's a fine cup of tea."
Maureen—"I brung up posh."

Me—I dream differently here.
Still Me—Maybe that's an imperative.
    Get up and write.

Buffalo Poems
New York '03

Sign Language

Dull with the day's slow-stepping hours,
Brought to light only by dreamed joys,
I listen for the door with its heavy hello,
Then a voice that devastates and thrills.

Even small homecomings can rush the heart.

I touch your face, hand-sliding down,
Thumbs brushing breasts,
A wrist-resting moment on your waist
And I pull you close.

Snow and street lamps dance to our nightly waltz.

Later, you move to your night rhythms above,
I to mine below, my pen in fits and stops.
But then I feel you like a bird's light shadow
Crossing the page, so I come to you . . . again.

Lovers look for signs, diviners of sorts.

Song to This Stage of Life

If the whole world is a stage
And my part bit, or broad,
I can embrace my role,
And play it to a packed house, or to you, alone.

But why are the lover's sighs
Or the wise man's words
Played on such a narrow stage
For just a brief scene, not for eternity or even near?

Yet the Fool—that script!
Plays before vast audiences, or just vastly before you,
Prompters never allowing a missed line,
A missed step, or entrance, or exit.

In aging I turn to show my mask
And await critical acclaim, playing the fool all too well!

Spring Training

We stood facing the other,
gloves oiled in the weeks
before we drove south
to burn and play
in the Carolina sun.

You, blond hair tucked beneath
a red cap, pounding small fist
into tan leather,
and me, not so much hair,
above a red face,
rubbing the new white ball
with the sweat of the hot day.

You stood, HoHo's garage door
your backstop for the missed balls
that might roll for what would be
forever for your small legs.
(He peeks from the window
to watch his first grandson,
you unaware, but I know he's there.)

I, a mere ten steps away,
half to the street,
confident of my glove,
made the first toss, from somewhere
between the shoulder and the ear,
not so confident of your glove,
more a dart than a baseball,
aimed to help you catch.

Yet it stuck deep in the webbing,
proof of the power that you had rubbed
hard into leather while snow
still fell outside your window.

Your return throw had zip,
even then, more than that
found in the arm of the boy
you left behind in the fall,
when leaves crunched in colors
beneath our sneakered feet
the last time we had played catch
before placing ball and gloves
to sleep through the hand-stinging months.

Spring training, now, we called it,
and we began to count
catches without a drop,
stabs without an errant throw.

I remember we laughed
when we reached twenty.
Twenty was a lot, we thought,
but we stayed in the sun that first day
and reached seventy-five.
(We stayed in the sun that first day
UNTIL we reached seventy-five.)

Then you looked at me with blue eyes,
holding the ball somewhere
above your shoulder, too dart-like,
as I offered the target,
my feet now all the way
in the street, a full ten steps back
from where we had started our game.

You looked at the ball,
and then at me.
You slammed it hard into the pocket
and we placed our gloves
under our arms.
And I placed my free arm
around your shoulder
and we walked into the house,
you knowing—and I hoping—
that our days would be filled
with games of catch until the numbers
rose into the thousands
and even tens of thousands.

And I still feel the ball
hit the glove
and you, sweaty and proud,
close by my side.

Song to This Day

Still, soft, serene day:
A wreathe of smoke, white like
The snow on trees and roofs
That touch the blue above,
Rises from across the way,
Everything pointing upward,
Freed to face the sky,
A breath of the newest year.

Reverence to the highest power—
Not for just this day as it unfolds
But for the unfolding of the house
As we stretch, and touch, and rise in ritual of renewal.

Not claiming a kiss, but gently touching you,
I pass to step into the day.

Thanatopsis for a Tabby

An Ode on a Friend's Cat Buried in Quebec
(With apologies to the Metaphysicians and their Conceits)

Sleep in your grave of humble sand and air
Sweetly, though no marble columns grace this spot.
Pause here Pilgrim, pet Pussy, gray Kitty—pause here,
Praised by the depthless universe.

Over the treetops I sing you this song,
Over the rippling lakes, over the cliffs and fields.
In the day and night, seamless now in death,
You slink and stretch in dreams of hunts and tender touches.

And stooping feline angels,
From cat-nippy clouds unseen,
Carry you to curl on couch magnificent:
For us one cat less; for you one world less—
Both free to float on the all-loving
    Whispering wave of memory . . .

Song to Night Fears

When Darkness tries the latch of my Heart,
Its faint tap, tap, tapping stirring me
From dreams of pebbled brooks
And rippled lakes and glittered seas,

My quiverings the dark hours entreat
For light to drive the shadow
Beyond the place of dreams.

My Soul, a childish thing that strays,
Then fears that which it beckons,
Needs only to light the torch
Of tender thoughts of you —

I have set you apart, a flame to light,
To heat, to heal my fears and my doubts
When Darkness tries the latch of my Heart.

A Small A.M. Poem for Lucie

I have seen you stop
'Neath shadows of trees
And bring sunlight
To the shade.

To a Cultured Friend

A voice from another country,
calm yet bound tightly
like a slinky or a phone cord,
proclaimed her Selfness:

"A life should be palpable
like a fucking coconut
or like a pebble-bottomed
mountain stream—gurgling yet mute.

"Let me fill the air with oaths to Self—
'Calooh! Callay!' No matter
that the words have no
Momes or Toves."

I stepped back,
fearful to occupy the space
of her words.
It must be madness, I thought.
Or she's British.

Reunion '67

So now I sing as I move toward my past,
penning verse without notes, song without sound.

Should my hymn be the blues
for those whose faces stay hidden
in the mist, for those who couldn't
keep pace with the living?

Or should it be accordion music?
Not the Zydeco but the polka tune
squeezing into my sleep when I've had
too many pretzels and too many beers.

(My nightmare is filled with sloe gin fizzes,
quart Schlitzes and ham sandwiches from the knife
of Mama Louie . . . but it doesn't frighten me;
I awaken strangely comforted . . . though bloated.)

The humming, not quite a melody yet,
gives way to images of a twelve-year-old
Little Leaguer, and of winding paths
home through Pine Woods Park

which by day seems far too small for a
boy whose world needs scope and breadth,
yet by night seems a looming darkness with waiting
Road Vultures straddling darker Harleys;

of street dances and necking parties;
of mattresses in damp concrete pool rooms

with stained ticking of love and near love—
It was so easy then, life at half price!

Our world was of squeaks and rollers—
no politics beyond the thickness of our socks.
Boys could pound their chests
and girls could pretend they were impressed.

But the beating chests gave way to the
beating of blades above the jungle
and our fetish for keeping score found us
counting our own and we wept adult tears.
(In our new world of desert fears
who could think there was so much moisture?)

The growing murmur of voices,
some rare fooling in my head—
storming sneering whining,
laughing loving winning:
The dull babble of youth filters
through all I've done and all I've known.

After compassing the world—some seeking, some drifting,
some flexing and growing, some repenting and submitting,
some conforming and confessing . . . but all changing—
we take a breath and look to the past,
inventing what might have been or never was
to escape being always locked in the moment.

Uprooting is a controlled explosion
that allows us to re-compose the parts—
though some lost to fate, and others to memory—
to prettify the past in a ritual of reunion.

What We Hear When We Think About Love

Strains of Country, of Rock, even of Rap
quiet the pen.
And sound now fills the head—
no longer just the ear.
And the page
stares empty, a frightful pause
before another song begins.

For every "Like a Falling Star from
heaven's blue, one moment bright
then lost from view," is a
"Aaallll I've ever wanted . . . was a
love ta be true."

Yelping, yelling, rapping.

In the mean time—

Last night I reached to slide
my fingers beneath the cotton
band to touch your side,
crossing miles of flannel fields
("In Flannel Fields the Poppies grow . . .")
to feel the warmth of your skin,
to let you know through your sleep
that I was there, will always be there:
"Don't worry Baby; ain't nuthin' new,
that's just love sneakin' up on you."

In darkness I wander,
drawn to the sweet curve of your side
trembling, needful, yet fearful
of the rebuke in the night;
yet I know, in light, you're there,
waiting for the touch, the soft word:
"You need a man who'll treat you
like a woman . . . rock steady, just me and you."

The music stops, the house sleeps.
I hear you turn in bed, hear your shoulder,
your face, your hair move against the pillow —
all soundless in the night;
it's something a lover knows, feels,
hears without the ear, much like the
songs in his head.

Soon I will reach across the bed
to slide my hand to touch your side.
And, as if perfumed poppies
gently close my lids, I sleep.

Letter to Self . . .
and a Response

"Hey Kid,
you're not twenty-five anymore.
So stop the gushy stuff
and focus on regret
and fear and . . .
you know,
stuff like that."

OK:
I regret that fear
rarely enters my mind
when all I really
want is to write
a poem that will
get me laid.

"Well, that's better—
still a romantic,
but a hopeless one."

Circe's Warning

Lashed to the spar, song in my ear,
I scream warnings to the rhythmed
Movements braced on deafened benches.

"Better to face death now!" I cry,
"Than to drag this sick life forward
In step with fate and time and text!"

They've read the script: they pull me on
Until the notes sink down beneath
The wake, replaced by silent tears.

It would have been a taste of life
To hit the rocks and wade the surf,
To meet the feathered breasts and beaks.

You could have told my story then—
A story of love, not regret.

Buffalo: February 1st . . . or 12th . . . or April 7th!

Another Yukon morning—
whiskey coffee, whiskey batter,
fire banked high
against . . . against . . .
against the reality that
the Yukon
is thousands of miles
safely to the Northwest.

Outside SUVs
deliver Starbucks
on plowed
roads to cabin-fevered
accountants and ophthalmologists
who eyeball the shrinking
woodpiles beside their
family-roomed fireplaces,
counting backwards
as they place each log
neatly . . . neat . . . ne . . . n.

Going, going . . .

but not gone for the
hard-wood delivery truck
arrives just behind
the Starbuck run,
and double-latte-mochaed

daughters hold the
doors as Dave
saves the day
and drops a cord or so he says
on the floors
and takes the checks
with a thanks
and returns to his forest
which he can't see
for the smoke
that rises above
the suburbs that now
grow as his woodlot shrinks
and he thinks just
two more Yukonish winters
and Florida beckons.

Back home
I flap another jack,
stare into the fire,
and swig
right
from
the
bottle.

Cabin fever—Catch it.

Tying a Poem

With thread and hair and feather
I dress the hook, gripped in vice.
With wrap and turn and dub
a fly takes shape—only a fake, I'm afraid.
But when I cast into stream
and it falls lifeless to the flow,
I can only hope it's mistaken
for something dropped by
Nature's hand and not by mine,
clumsy and nervous.
Sometimes it fools
and a streak from below hits it hard
or sucks it softly from the film
and I know I've worked magic
for at least one uncritical eye.
Often it drifts untouched,
perhaps even unseen,
until it sinks below the riffle
or until it catches on stone or twig
and I'm forced to break it loose,
to begin again to add
hackle to hook, quill to dun,
hoping, again, to fool
with my artless offering.

Winter's Secret

Winter calls for Love
As do the other
Seasons
But more so.

For Spring boasts of Hope,
Racing forward, eyes
Looking
Everywhere.

Summer, Confident,
Too passes quickly
Never
Truly "here."

Fall—season of Fear—
Looks ahead with eyes
Downcast,
Fearing death.

But Winter! Secret Strength
From lovers held close
Burning
Their own Fires!

Old as I am now,
Young still I approach
Winter's
Nights to Burn with you.

No budding trees,
No lingering suns,
No dying leaves
Sitting in judgment.

Just
You.

Confession

I have a confession:

Bless me Father
(and you bless me too,
those I've deceived
leading you to think
me harmless, just another
jester)
I have secrets
(and secret thoughts
that could become secrets
had I the time
or the inclination
to act)
that would challenge
sensibilities,
that would shock
those who know me,
those who think me
meek and weak.

Lives are private places . . .
with visiting hours.
Lives are rough and disturbing . . .
edited for television.

I was told that,
told to live quiet . . .
and forget.

So now I write
Confessional poetry,
Church booths no longer
Enough.

Reconstructing Terpy
(May 15, 2003)

We sit on the edge of the bed,
box of history—your history—between us:
Of course it's our story too,
the moments and fragments of moments
we shared and share again, now,
passing pictures and papers
from a mother's hand to a father's.

We touch each and search for
your childhood in the folds
of yellowed clippings and crayoned cards,
of snapshots and self-portraits.

Digging downward,
archaeologically from today
to the days before and then the years,
we unearth your past,
gently dusting each
with smiles and tears.

First a college proof.
("Eyes clear and spirit strong"—
words of a father
proud of you at twenty.)
Pressed against pink sunglasses
a photo of you checking
the authenticity of your gold medal.
(Always the skeptic!)

Scavenger hunter, scavenger
of treasure on big trash day;
heroine of poetry: "The Yard,"
The Geisha," "The Fire,"
a beautiful young girl
rubbing Eleanor's feet.

Your NOTHING BOOK:
"I'd rather laugh with the sinners
than cry with the saints!"
Letter home regarding play: "Have a role.
I'm Gloria—strong kinda slutty person."

[Dad's thought: Glad it's a camp letter,
not a college one!]

Hats! Hats! Hats!
Always the Hats!
"I can wear them all,"
you seem to say,
and you wear them well.

SUMMER ACHIEVEMENT BOOKLET:
White Sail, Canoeing, Kayaking, Swimming, Diving.
You dive into everything, Mrs. Smee:
even he Sings your praises—
for using, not just memorizing,
your 'power words.'

You booked your feelings:
"I was honest when my Mom asked who *writted*
On the floor and I said Me."
Fifth grade: White dress and not-so-white cast.
"World! You break me up, piece by piece.
But I'm gonna be stronger in the broken places."
And you are.

And I see that strength
as you lift the axe fireside,
and dance with Monk,
and stand at bat,
always with those eyes
anchored to task.

Ah, there's Monk's
Christmas stocking
(looking oddly like
a sock gone missing in 1985)
and a bib proclaiming "1"
and a drawing of a dock
and that must be me
fishing off the end —
all scraps of yesterday.

And Mom and I dig,
like miners, into your life.
Or like we're peeling
an onion, layer by layer,
but the tears are tears
of joy for all those times
and the times between those times.

This family reunion in a box
shows you grow
wise and sure.
And we sit here,
wearing our gestures,
holding you in hands and hearts.
Even in pictures and papers
it's a good thing,

to hold you near,
late into the night,
sitting on the edge of our bed,
with you between us.

Of Slate and Cordwood

Lifeless picture of slate and cordwood,
Grass matted in dried carpet
Against still branches
And even stiller fence.

February: backdrop for images
Dull and dead for the man whose
Muse shares the pallet
And the brush with the lifeless.

But for the living artist—
The landscape shaper
Tugging and pushing his
Three-boundaried world
Outward from the flat landscape
Of the eye and the mind—
The cold stone and rough wood,
The crunching of foot to ground,
The clicking boughs, the falling fence
Give motion to the senses
And depth to a world otherwise
Flat and silent and still.

Resolutions

When my ship comes in,
I'll be ready this time,
Sea-bag packed, shouldered
To make quick step to deck.

Shore leave—fifty years—
Has left me soft in limb
And hard in habit
But eager for sea-change.

Out there in the fog
It feels its way to port;
Behind I'm tugged by
Thoughts of harbor pleasure.

Lot-like, I peer seaward, afraid to look back;
Then I shrug, turn, trudge the hill once again to Sodom.

A Conscious Fancy

The house is quiet now.
Somewhere above Rome
you drowse perhaps,
dreaming of being near me
as I sleep, or
dreaming of running from me
as I chase you, or
dreaming of dancing on the table
as I spray champagne upward
to your laughing hands, or
dreaming of whatever you dream away from me:
It's mere whimsy, you see,
that places me in your dream.

But awake, here, I am free to wander
beyond the manners and customs
tossed about in dreamscapes,
which are little more
(and more often much less!)
than a night's replay of past days'
dances and delights
edited by unconscious fancy
to make you think that dreams
are fresh and free.

So in my wandering
I think of sins to discover,
deeds to delight,
passions for daylight and for night,
spells to cast on you
yet undreamt, unheard, unwritten, unknown.

When next you meet my eyes with yours
you can only guess what we've done,
where we've gone,
just as I can only guess, now,
your dreams, somewhere over Rome.

The difference is,
dreams are mostly done—
while awake here I think
on that yet undone.

Did You Feel My Touch in Mexico?

I sit here, elbows on bended knees,
Before a fire imagined,
Staring into the flames,
Feeling the warmth of your absent love.

I stretch my palms toward the orange heat,
And your breasts lean to meet them.
Just so! Separation—
Minds whisp'ring canvas calls to the brush.

Make your marks upon me while I'm still,
Lost in dreams carnal and calm;
My nakedness—reverie—
Your strokes cover . . . soft, silent, tender.

Your art is to reach across distance
As I search for you in flick'ring thought.

Written for Play

The loon over lakes and trees seeks his home,
the black mink to his beneath the bank,
and I, no less wild, to my quiet nest return
to find rest beside you:
    You, with your look as you sleep,
    Your legs that stir lusts in me
    that never die—only nap, as it were,
    and then for only the briefest hour.

So let me place this morning verse before you,
knowing you will see it for roses and wine
from a shameless pen, bent on little more
than speaking silent passion,
from one who loves, to one loved.

At the Poussin Exhibit

Venus gave birth to a
Monstrously endowed Priapus.
Freud would understand
How he got that way,
But the woman from Ohio
Who stood in front of me
Squinting, hand on jaw,
Mouth covered as if in shock,
Could not:
"Did you see this, Ed?
How could such a little
Baby have such a big wee wee?"
Ed was looking at the nipples
Of the tittering goddesses,
Especially at those of Venus
Who reclined on the garden bench.
Ed too knew the answer
But kept silent.